OVERCOMING PAIN: STEPPING INTO PURPOSE

Jazlyn Jones

Overcoming Pain: Stepping into Purpose

RiverHouse Publishing, LLC
1509 Madison Avenue
Memphis, TN 38104

Copyright © 2018 by Jazlyn Jones

All rights reserved. No part of this book may be reproduced, stored in a retrieval system or transmitted in any form or by any means without written permission of the Publisher, excepting brief quotes used in reviews.

All **RiverHouse Publishing, LLC** Titles, Imprints and Distributed Lines are available at special quantity discounts for bulk purchases for sales promotions, premiums, fund-raising and educational or institutional use.

First RiverHouse, LLC Trade Paperback Printing: 10/30/2018

ISBN: 978-0-9988108-9-8

Printed in the United States of America

This book is printed on acid-free paper.

www.riverhousepublishingllc.com

This book is dedicated to those who have gone through some painful situations. Although you've suffered, purpose is waiting. Your beginning doesn't determine your ending. Let's overcome our pain and step into purpose together.

Acknowledgments

God,
I love you. Thank you for dying so that I may have life. Thank you for considering me. Thank you for choosing me. You looked beyond my brokenness, and my mistakes just to place me in my purpose. You allowed me to grow for someone else. You believed in me when I had given up on myself. You called me your daughter, a royal priesthood. You never judged my actions, but you loved me unconditionally. I'll forever spread your goodness. I'll forever help others overcome their pain and reach their purposed place. You're amazing.
Thank you for life!

To my mother:
Your death caused me to live. Although it took a process to arrive at my purposed place, I thank you. Everything that I endured after your transition was all for a purpose. You would always profess that I was going to be great as a child. I never knew what that fully meant but now I can stand boldly and say thank you for speaking life over me. I'll continue to make you proud. I pray that I'll be half the mother you were to my siblings and me. Forgive me for attempting to replace your love with everything else. I love you forever, Mommy.

To my father:
Although you didn't understand everything that I experienced in those earlier years, thank you for being there. Most times, I'm sure you didn't even have the words to say but just your presence during those times made it much better. You're the epitome of a father. Thank you for never judging me. Thank you for loving me. I'll continue to make you proud. Love you, twin.

To my bonus mother:
Forgive me for the anger that I had against you during those earlier years. Forgive me for holding a grudge and not wanting to accept another mother. I thank God that our relationship has taken a complete turn. I thank God that you stepped up to help my father. I thank you for not giving up. I thank you for learning how to love me. I love you, Mom!

To my siblings and nieces:
You've witnessed my entire transition. You've seen me at my worst and now are witnessing me at my best. I thank God for allowing me to grow through someone else, especially you all. Everything I've experienced, I pray that you'll never have to encounter. I pray that I can be the example you all need. I'll always be here for you. I love you all!

To my spiritual parents:
Thank you for covering me. Thank you for loving me back to life. You guys have made a huge impact in my life. I'll forever thank God for placing you two individuals in my life. During some of my worst

seasons, you never gave up on me. Thank you for getting in the pit just to pull me out. Thank you for not letting me give up on myself. I'm forever grateful for you all

Table of Contents

Chapter One: Introduction 1

Chapter Two: The Past... 2

Chapter Three: The Pain.. 6

Chapter Four: The Process 13

Chapter Five: HIS Plan 21

Chapter Six: Stepping into Purpose 24

Chapter Seven: Completion 37

Chapter One: Introduction

PURPOSE:

: // something created or for which something exists.

: // an assignment that God has created specifically to fulfill on earth.

We've all dealt with pain before. Pain has the ability to change you, grow you, or destroy you. It's your choice to decide which route you'll take in life. In my situation, pain pushed me into my purpose.

Throughout this book, I decided to use personal testimonials not to glorify myself but to glorify God. In this book, I purposely magnified painful phases of my life to help awaken the purpose that lies beneath the pain within. I want to remind you that you aren't alone; pain isn't permanent and there's purpose in every situation that you've had to endure.

This is my story.

Chapter Two: The Past

THE BEGINNING

Growing up, I was an Army brat. My father had been serving in the military for years. Within the Army, there are various changes. Relocating has to be one of the leading issues. In the year of 2003, my dad had to move overseas. Our family then moved back to my mother's hometown in the state of Mississippi. Years later, I remember this exact memory. We were living in a three-bedroom apartment and this day was quite strange. Peeking through my mother's door, I watched her crying on the floor. At the time, I was unsure of what was happening, but as I grew older, I understood what transpired during that emotional experience. My parents had decided to get a divorce. Although, I love both of my parents that was a painful experience - from being raised in a traditional household to being separated without full understanding.

My father has been supportive throughout my entire life. Although he is supportive, his absence in the household those remaining years, created my perception on relationships and affection. Growing up I desired to witness that unconditional love within the household. I witnessed men come into our lives and disappear. I witnessed the hurt that my mother desperately tried to hide. I witnessed the arguments that occurred throughout the nights. I witnessed the pain and I developed the perception that happiness would always be associated with pain.

Years later, my father retired from the military and moved back to Mississippi. After all, of those years apart, my parents agreed that I could move in with my father. Relocating from familiarity to a new environment was scary. Although I had to get adjusted to the new environment, living with my father was exciting. Our relationship began to grow. Weekends were reserved for dates with my father. Each day in my father's presence was a present. Although the new environment was relaxed, I begin having struggles in school. I was exposed to things far beyond my maturity. As a teenager, I felt that I couldn't confide in my father about the exposure. Therefore, I remained silent. Then after two years, I had to move back with my mom.

I was then entering a new high school. Another new school. Another new environment and more exposure. I gained friends who were already engaging in sexual activity, skipping school, and partying. This was new. Although my mom wasn't aware, I just wanted to fit in. I wanted to engage in activities that all of my friends were engaging in. Therefore, I begin making some of the worse decisions.

THE TRANSISTION

Soon after, my entire life changed. My mom was diagnosed with breast cancer. I felt broken and confused. I was young, and I needed my mother. We began to visit doctors – which became a part of our routine. We went through surgeries, and radiation, and we had finally beat cancer. Months later, we continued treatments and the doctors found cancer cells traveling throughout her body. The process began again. Our family has always believed in prayer, so we believed the report of the Lord. Although we were praying, things grew worse. I witnessed my mother battle with breast cancer and continue to work tiredly. I watched her bedroom transform into a hospital room. I watched this vibrant individual transform into this individual who couldn't respond to me. This was the hardest pill to swallow.

I was a teenager. I'll always remember those dreading words. "Your mother has 48 hours left to live." June 2, 2011 God called her home. In seconds, my life had been stripped away from me. The life that I was used to was destroyed. The person I needed for guidance was taken away from me. My mother, my covering, my friend. The fact that I was so young, I would not only have to experience life without my mother, but I would have to move away.

"Numb, angry, depressed, and confused" were just a few of my emotions.

Chapter Three: The Pain

THE AFTERMATH

This pain began to change me. I was depressed. I began to question God. I wanted to know why he allowed this to happen to me. I walked around full of laughter but when I was alone, this empty feeling continued to overtake me. I had to find activities that would keep me happy. I remember the first time that I engaged in sexual activity. He made me feel valued. He expressed his love for me and I had his full attention.

Although, it was a temporary feeling, I wanted to feel that type of love again. I started to desire the attention from others because I desperately wanted to fill this empty feeling. I desired materialistic things because it would keep me happy. I had traded my happiness for something that could walk away, be stolen, or lost. I adopted this new cycle, but my happiness was conditional.

The separation had left a huge void, which I desired to be filled.

I was hopeless and lost mentally and emotionally. I had fallen victim to looking for the fulfillment through young men. Nothing worked. This mentality kept me in the place of brokenness. I needed a way out.

Note:

Don't look for internal fulfillment from a physical being. When we begin to set expectations for people, we are setting ourselves up for failure and heartbreak. Expectations can create chaos because although a person has "potential" we expect them to fulfill duties they aren't capable of. Trust that God is able to do all things.

BATTLE BETWEEN THE WORLD AND THE WORD

Finally, I graduated from high school. It was the happiest day of my life. I felt that I had finally accomplished something. I had been accepted to the University of Mississippi. I thought this may be a new beginning. I may finally become content and happy with life. I was wrong.

Excessive partying and more freedom. I consistently engaged in different tasks to keep my focus off the feeling of loneliness, the past, and most of all, the pain.

Family and friends couldn't identify because I painted a pretty picture of perfection. I quoted scriptures, I was faithful in church, but I didn't have a relationship with God.

There is a major difference between a relationship with God and attending church. The church is a physical building where individuals gather. A relationship with God is allowing Him to reside in you. You're the church!

It was the summer going into my junior year of college. I surrendered to God. I had run away from my assignment long enough. I had been hurt long enough. I had been portraying fake happiness long enough.

Although my parents raised us in church, this time I surrendered to God. I gave Him full access and control over my heart, my mind, and my life.

Things changed drastically.

Life in God was great. I accepted my assignment in ministry. I finally had peace. That's when things began to shift.

When you allow God to take full control over your life, don't expect to be comfortable.

Everything began to shift in my life including my family, friends, and finances.

"Why is this happening?"

"God, I surrendered."

When you begin to surrender yourself to God, the process won't be easy. Not only will God test what you profess, the anointing on your life will attract attacks. For those reading this, whatever you're facing, don't give up. Your situation won't always be this way. The process is hard, but the promise is worth it. Think about Jesus and everything he had to endure. He endured being spit on. He endured being beaten. He endured so that we may have life.

THE RESIDUE OF THE CYCLE

I knew I was this strong woman of God until what I thought I overcame, surfaced back up. Here I am again... back in the same place of stagnation due to the inner battle of what I'm presented with and what I'm accustomed to.

Reflecting back, I know many still have this problem.

Think about a scar. We get hurt, we experience that pain, and we may bleed. Then we undergo the healing process. As a child, when the scar begins to heal I would always fiddle with it. This would cause pain and bleeding, which would start the healing process over. That's similar to how we are today! Whatever caused you pain, grow through your healing process. Don't return to that pain. Don't return to that brokenness. Don't return to those old habits. Allow yourself to fully heal.

When God blocks it, leave it. Dysfunction doesn't have to be normal in your life. Peace, prosperity, and true happiness is your portion.

Don't be afraid to break the cycle.

Don't be afraid to break the generational curse.

Don't be afraid to beat the odds.

The world needs exactly what God has placed inside of you. The ministry, the book, the nonprofit organization. We need it.

Allow your pain to be the fuel for your purpose. God has allowed everything that you've experienced. He allowed you to grow through someone else. Don't give up because it seems as if the battle is too tough.

I'm reminded of Job. He was described as an upright and blameless man. He was wealthy, had a wife, children, and livestock. He didn't sin against God, but Satan was prowling looking for someone to devour when God responded, "Did you consider my servant Job?"

He lost everything, and his body began to be attacked but through God, he gained it all back double. This story encourages me because you may feel that you have been tormented long enough. You may not understand the reason for the struggle that you're currently experiencing. Remember that He considered Job. He allowed this, therefore be encouraged because the enemy's power is only limited under God's authority. Embrace your process, grow through this season.

PRAYER OVER PAIN

Dear God,

For those who may be suffering in silence. For those who may feel that they'll never be happy. For those who may be contemplating suicide. God, I speak that you'll begin to release your peace over their lives. God, I pray that you'll strengthen them for this journey. I pray against depression. God, I pray that they won't fall victim to looking for love in the wrong places. I pray that you'll allow your love to overtake them. I pray that you'll fill each and every empty void. God, I pray that their past will no longer torment them. I pray that their pain will no longer hinder them. I pray that you're mending hearts, families, and marriages. I pray that each person will begin to get in alignment with your word. God, I pray that prosperity is their portion. Begin to shift our focus now.

We love you. We honor you.
Amen!

Chapter Four: The Process

Process
pro – cess
noun

1. a series of actions or steps taken in order to achieve a goal.

THE PROPOSAL

Finally, I'm back in that place of peace. I met this guy; he was different. Therefore, I allowed myself to remove the barriers and love again. We dated, we both were in ministry, and everything was perfect. In September 2016, he proposed. Of course, I said YES! I immediately began planning the wedding of a lifetime. I said yes to the dress. I had a beautiful bridal shower, a bachelorette party, and I was preparing to become a wife.

Things changed. We soon realized that our relationship and becoming one wasn't as easy. Financial issues, internal issues, and past issues arose.

Then there was the **separation**.

Broken, humiliated and hurt. How could I go from happily engaged to single? How could I explain this to family, friends, and my bridal party? How could I refund all of the dresses and gifts? How did our relationship become toxic?

I had to cry at night but smile and be social throughout the day. I had to wear my ring just to avoid questions. Internally, I cringed when someone asked, *was I ready?*

I had to pretend that I wasn't in pain.

Once again, I had to pick up my mask of perfection.

Thinking, *why was my life full of pain? Why couldn't I just be happy and content?*

PICKING UP THE PIECES

It was June and I hadn't found a job yet. You would think with a bachelor's degree, you'll have millions of positions available. I was being denied for not having enough experience to not having enough credentials. Soon, I finally was hired but the pay wasn't what I expected. Here I am driving an hour back and forth to work. Excited yet feeling defeated. Faithful yet drained. I can vividly remember calling my dad and telling him, I would have to move closer to my job. Internally, I was afraid because I would have to take on more responsibilities and more bills. Although I was afraid, I kept my faith.

During this season, I had to learn how to be alone again. I remember trying to fill the void once again. I remember leaving one job, running to the next. I remember calling and telling the finance company that they would have to just take my car. I remember deciding which bills I could pay. I remember quoting scriptures to give me strength. Most of all, I remember the pain that I felt. It was during that season that the pain was preparing me. The pain was building me. Then, I didn't understand why I had to go through those difficult seasons, but it was molding me for greater. Therefore, if you're currently feeling defeated, rejoice knowing that God chose you for greater. He's using your "it" to strengthen and mold you for more. Your current pain was only created to prepare and promote you for your purpose. You've come too far. Don't give up! You're stepping into the greatest years of your life. Overcome the pain and tap into your power.

You've sown in tears. You've been faithful. You've remained immovable. It's time for you to reap!

"Let us not grow weary or become discouraged in well doing, for at the proper time we will reap, if we don't faint." Galatians 6:9 AMP

NOTE TO SINGLES:

1. Trust God's timing.
2. Don't allow social media to rush your process. Comparing your life to someone based on pictures can create issues within you.
3. Marriage is beautiful but don't allow it to be your only goal. While waiting, continue to work on you.
4. Love yourself. A significant other or material things won't make you happy. Happiness starts within.
5. Don't look for internal fulfillment from a physical being. Only God has the power to fulfill each desire of your heart.
6. Identify your purpose and fulfill it. The solution to your problems isn't marriage, a degree, or more money. The solution is allowing the void to be filled. Filled by God. Filled with his everlasting and unconditional love.

Singleness isn't discipline from God, but a blessing. Grow through your single season. Grow with God. Grow as an individual and become the best version of yourself. Marriage won't solve your pain or your past. Embrace the season God has placed you in. You can't afford to be distracted. Purpose is awaiting!

THE PROCESS

As you think about your process, be encouraged that you're taking the necessary steps to become better. Don't skip or rush your process, because the process is necessary. Think about your process as cooking a meal. I remember cooking my first meal. I began frying the fish and cooking spaghetti. I had been watching others cook this meal for years; therefore, I abandoned the instructions. Dinner was finally done, and I began eating. After my first bite, I remember spitting the food out everywhere. Because I abandoned the steps given to cook a successful meal, the result was failure. Think about the process of your life. If we skip or rush the process, we may step out prematurely or end in failure. Don't neglect the process. It's during the process that God is preparing you for your purpose.

I'm sure you're reading this book and saying to yourself... *I understand that the process is necessary but how can I overcome the pain of what I've experienced?*

1. **Prayer** is simply a conversation connecting you with God. We can overcome pain through prayer. Through prayer, God can begin to heal, build, and strengthen us. Through prayer, we begin to deepen our relationship with God and become a part of Christ.

"Therefore, if any man be in Christ, he is a new creature: old things are passed away; behold, all things are become new."
2 Corinthians 5:17

You're made new through Him. Begin to walk into your newness. You were created for greater. Don't allow your pain to hinder your purpose. There's need for you.

2. **Grow through your pain**. You're in the process and remember there's beauty in growing through what you thought would destroy you. You may be feeling uncomforta-

ble and slight pressure but it's only growing pains. God is shifting your circumstances. No longer will you dwell over the pain you've experienced but let's shift into how we can overcome what we've experienced.

3. **Shift your focus**. Begin to discover what makes you happy. Begin to identify your passion. If we continually focus on moving forward, the thought or reminder of pain begins to dissolve. Whatever you feed, grows. Begin to feed on the positive and grow purposeful.

4. **Purpose**. There's purpose in your pain. Therefore, overcome pain by understanding that God didn't create us to go through pain, but He allows us to experience pain. When we experience this pain, He knows that we're equipped and strong enough to overcome it. After overcoming pain, we must encourage the next person through our story and allow God to be glorified. Therefore, you may not understand the pain now, but the purpose will be revealed through it.

5. You may be saying to yourself "You don't understand the depth of my pain?" I don't

but God does, because we all deal with pain differently. If necessary, **seek mentorship, accountability, and/or counseling.** We won't continue to suffer in silence. We can't continue to build others, while neglecting our brokenness. We can't continue to save the world but lose ourselves. You shall live through this.

Chapter Five: HIS Plan

Plan:
/plan/
God's strategic proposal for achieving or fulfilling something.

Now that we understand the process, become confident knowing that everything was a part of His plan. God had a plan for our lives before we were formed in our mother's womb. Everything we've experienced from tragedy to triumph was a part of His perfect plan for our life. He died that we may have life and life more abundantly.

Abundantly means having more than enough. Do you understand that he wants us to live in a continuous overflow? We weren't created to live a mediocre life. The plan you desired was mediocre compared to what God has for you. We serve a God that has a strategic plan for you to be prosperous. He knows the desires of your heart. Allow Him to manifest in your life.

"For I know the plans I have for you," declares the Lord, "plans to prosper you and not to harm you, plans to give you hope and a future."
Jeremiah 29:11

As I write, I'm reminded of a painful story that ended in God's perfect plan. Joseph was the youngest son of Jacob. He was favored by his father; therefore, he made Joseph a special robe of many colors. His brothers grew jealous because of his special treatment.

Then one day, Joseph had a dream. He revealed the dream to his brothers and they replied, "Do you think you are better than us that we would bow to you?" His brothers then plotted to kill him but eventually sold him to the people heading to Egypt. They reported to the father Jacob, and falsely stated that an animal had killed his younger son.

Joseph then arrived as a slave, but the Lord was with him. He had done everything right, so Potiphar gave him access to be a helper by giving him authority over everything he owned.

Then Potiphar's wife lied about Joseph to her husband and he was placed in jail. While in jail, no one could explain the dream to the Pharaoh but Joseph. Joseph explained to him that "God is warning you.

There will be seven years when nothing will grow and there won't be any food for anyone." After explaining the dreams, the king released him and placed him in a higher position. Joseph had been placed over all of Egypt.

People were coming from all countries to buy food, even Joseph's brothers. The brothers all bowed to him because he was a person of high rank, just as he dreamed they would at the beginning. After a few meetings with his brothers, he revealed himself to his brothers. His brothers were afraid and apologetic. So his father, his brothers, and their families came to live in Egypt with Joseph, and they had all the food in the famine.

How amazing is it that although we suffer and experience great pain, God has a plan connected to it. I'm excited because God is about to release the biggest plot twist in your life. He is about to release favor in the midst of the famine. He's shifting you from being pitiful to powerful. He is setting you up for the greatest purposeful years of your life. Don't be discouraged how your story began. Your story shall end in purpose and prosperity.

God's plan > our plan.

Chapter Six: Stepping into Purpose

"For you created my inmost being; you knit me together in my mother's womb. I praise you because I am fearfully and wonderfully made; your works are wonderful, I know that full well."
Psalm 139:13-14

In the womb, we were destined for greatness. He created us for a special purpose and assignment. Although he created us for purpose, the enemy's motive is to kill, steal, and destroy. He wants to kill your destiny, steal your joy, and destroy your future. I have a confession. He wants you to forfeit your assignment; that's why he's been fighting you so hard. He doesn't want you to fulfill your purpose because it will cause a positive change. It will cause an impact. An impact to an individual, an impact to a nation, an impact to a community. He wants you to forfeit your purpose and dwell in that painful place. I speak with authority that even while reading you'll be motivated to walk into your destined place.

You've neglected your purpose long enough. You've felt inferior long enough. You've been stagnant far too long. Overcome the fear of failure.

"For God has not given us a spirit of fear, but of power and of love and of a sound mind."
2 Timothy 1:7

Allow your faith to override the fear within. He has already equipped us for everything that we'll experience. You have the power. Get in position.

I have great news! You're reading this book, which is an indication that there is still a purposeful life waiting. There's a nation that needs your vision, your idea, your business, your ministry. Reflecting back, I understand that the pain I dealt with was equipping me to handle the young women that would experience what I faced.

Losing my mother was shaping me to become a mentor to those who are experiencing grief. They need someone to show them they can survive. You're their hope. You may not have understood why you had to go through that traumatic situation.

You may not understand why that person had to walk away. You may not understand why you had to experience so much pain, but God loves and trusts you so much that he chose you. Remember the story of Job, which was told earlier. Yes, you've lost somethings but because you didn't give up your double is coming.

Even while you're reading, begin to repeat this.

"This is the last day I'll allow the pressure of my past to produce pity within my mind. I won't allow my pain to punk me out of my purpose. The promise and purpose over my life remains. Today, I'm deciding to overcome the pain and step into my God given purpose."

Some of you may not fully understand the steps to stepping into your purpose. As you begin to establish and walk into your purpose, you must begin to pray, find your identity, and identify your purpose.

1. Pray for direction, guidance, and understanding. God will begin to reveal your purpose through petitioning Him. If he has revealed your purpose, begin to ask God to guide your steps.

And I will do whatever you ask in My name, so that the Father may be glorified in the Son. If you ask Me anything in My name, I will do it.

John 14:13-14

2. Identity is simply finding and becoming who you're destined to be. This step can be very

important because learning your true identity provides an understanding for your purpose. You must know who you truly are before you can identify what you're called to. Many of us can't step into our purpose because we haven't asked God to reveal who we truly are. God can't use who you pretend to be. You can't continue to walk blindly and live up to the standards that people released over our life. You're more than just an individual on earth. Out of the millions of cells that don't reach the egg, God allowed YOU to be formed because He had purpose over your life before you were born. Do you understand that you're royalty to God – we are Queens and Kings in the eyes of God? You're chosen. Be encouraged because today is the last day you'll operate beneath the standard that God has for you.

"But you are a chosen people, a royal priesthood, a holy nation, God's special possession, that you may declare the praises of him who called you out of darkness into his wonderful light."
1 Peter 2:9

3. When you begin to walk into your purpose, you must identify and distinguish between your passion and your purpose. Your passion is simply a strong feeling or the fuel that lies within. Your passion is what drives you. You have a desire for it. Your purpose is what you were placed on earth to fulfill. Therefore, you may have a passion for it, but are you purposed to do it? Throughout life, we have one divine purpose, but many passions. I love that God is so amazing because even if they may differ, He allows us to fulfill our passion and purpose. Identify what God has for you and embrace the process to get to your purposed place. Your purpose shall bring glory to the Kingdom of God.

"For just as in one physical body we have many parts, and these parts do not all have the same function or special use, so we, who are many, are one body in Christ, and individually parts one of another. Since we have gifts that differ according to the grace given to us, each of us is to use them accordingly: if someone has the gift of prophecy, in proportion to the faith possessed; if service, in the act of serving, or he who teaches, in the act of teaching; or he who encourages, in the act of

encouragement; he who gives, with generosity; he who leads, with diligence; he who shows mercy, with cheerfulness."
Romans 12:4-8 AMP

When you begin to think about purpose, think about the physical body.

We all have different organs, tissues, and body parts that have a specific assignment. Each works together to help the body function successfully.

Our purpose is the same as well. God gives us each unique purposeful assignments and gifts that will continue to work together to make an impact on the earth. We're one body, many members.

"There are different kinds of gifts, but the same Spirit distributes them. There are different kinds of service, but the same Lord. There are different kinds of working, but in all of them and in everyone it is the same God at work."
1 Corinthians 12: 4-6 NIV

PURPOSEFUL PRAYER

Dear God,

We thank you for creating us. We thank you for everything that you've allowed in our lives. We thank you for giving us strength to live beyond the pain. We pray that you'll begin to speak to our hearts and minds regarding our purpose. Allow us to identify and understand your voice. God, I pray that you'll remove fear from our hearts. Allow us to shift from pain to purpose. From the pit to the palace. Allow us to break generational curses. Allow us to become who you've predestined us to be. Allow us to overcome every painful situation and step into our purpose. God, we thank you in advance for manifesting in our lives.

We truly love you. We honor you.

Amen!

WHAT'S YOUR PURPOSE?

"And the LORD answered me: "Write the vision; make it plain on tablets, so he may run who reads it."
Habakkuk 2:2

Chapter Seven: Completion

Completion:
//com - ple - tion
the action or process of finishing something.

I purposely wanted to end this book with Chapter 7. We've reflected on our pain, we're motivated for our purpose. Biblically, the number 7 stands for completion. The cycles are broken. Therefore, I'm declaring that we aren't just starting but we are finishing. This time we are completing....

Completing the book.
Completing the business plan.
Completing the degree.
Completing the application.
Completing the process.

We won't forfeit the process. We won't forfeit the assignment. We're growing somewhere. We're becoming who God has called us to be. We've experienced the pain but we're stepping into our purpose. As you're reading this, I want you to rejoice now that your pain wasn't meant to break you. I want you to finish this book and begin to activate your faith and walk into your purpose. **This is your confirmation.** You weren't meant to go through life with pain. There may be someone reading this who has lost hope. I pray that you begin to become like David. As the Amalekites had invaded, attacked, and burned Ziklag, they took the women captive and carried them away. As David and his men arrived, they were dismayed. And David asked the Lord, *shall I pursue after this troop? Shall I overtake them?*

And the Lord answered *pursue, overtake and without fail recover all.*

For each reader, it's time to "PURSUE, OVERTAKE AND RECOVER ALL." Recover everything that has been stripped away. Your joy, your happiness, your dreams, your family, your ministry, your life.

As we complete this book, begin to ask yourself, *Will I continually live in fear or allow faith to guide me? Will I continually dwell over painful situations or begin to walk into my purpose?*

"For we know that all things work together for the good of those who love God and are called according to His purpose." Romans 8:28

Therefore, the fight is fixed. You're already victorious and undefeated. Whatever you're facing is working for your good.

Although you're waiting, God is working. You can't give up because glory is connected to your purpose. A nation is waiting for your story. Your situation was only a setup. God has set you up for purpose on purpose. He knew that you would be at this very place in life. Rejoice because it wasn't meant to build you, nor break you! This is the last day you'll allow your pain to deter you from your purpose. Destiny awaits.

CLOSING PRAYER

Dear God,

I pray that as we finish this book, you'll begin to release the momentum, provisions, and fuel for our purpose. I pray that distractions and doubt won't delay our process. I speak that this time we are stepping into our purpose. God, for every reader, begin to awaken their spirit. Begin to order their steps. Begin to reveal our true identity. Allow us to become the person you've predestined us to be. We won't allow fear or doubt to stop us. We won't allow distractions to stop us. Begin to give us Godly insight. Allow our fire to be ignited now. We thank you for fresh wind.

We love you. We honor you.
Amen!

About the Author

Jazlyn Jones, is an author, founder of Purposeful Styles, charismatic leader and a graduate of the University of Mississippi. Jazlyn is from the great state of Mississippi.

During her teenage years, her mother transitioned and gained her wings due to a lengthy battle with breast cancer. Due to her faith and embodiment of Phil 4:13 "I can do all things through Christ who strengthen me," Jazlyn overcame this difficult season and persevered. The absence of her mother awakened her fire for Christ, which led to Jazlyn desiring to share her testimony and impact those surrounded around her.

Jones states that her ultimate purpose in life is to "evolve daily, fulfill her God given purpose and impact the lives of others, especially young women."

She believes that her drive to impact lives was the foundation for birthing out her business Purposeful Styles and releasing her book "Overcoming Pain; Stepping into Purpose.

Website:
Facebook: Jazlyn Jones
Email: JazlynjJones@gmail.com

www.ingramcontent.com/pod-product-compliance
Lightning Source LLC
Chambersburg PA
CBHW022121090426
42743CB00008B/957